# Draw What You Do

Bill Flury

## ACKNOWLEDGEMENTS

Many thanks for the inspiration and help from all of my process improvement colleagues. Special thanks to Rick Gibson, Twyla Courtot and Chris Fristad. They are my Experts and we have truly built the process in this Book together.

Diana Fraser provided essential design and editing advice. The illustrations were produced with the aid of software applications by Wordle.com and Caricature Software.

Special thanks to my Mary Flury who has patiently supported me in so many ways throughout our many years together and especially through the gestation of this product.

Copyright 2013 Bill Flury

All rights reserved.

ISBN-13: 978-1494275181

ISBN-10: 149427518X

# Draw What You Do
## A Practical Approach to Process Improvement
============================================================

This book is for you. It is a guide for you to use to improve the processes you follow. It provides a practical, step by step approach that will help you see, understand, and agree with your co-workers on what you do, how best to do it, and how to do it better.

The approach avoids the jargon and obscure acronyms of the formal process improvement programs or any requirements for extensive and expensive documentation. The steps involved have been distilled from over 100 implementations, and they have been proven to work.

If you do as suggested you will find relief from your day-to-day work headaches, minimize your crises, and make your work experience more enjoyable – maybe even go so far as to make it fun.

============================================================

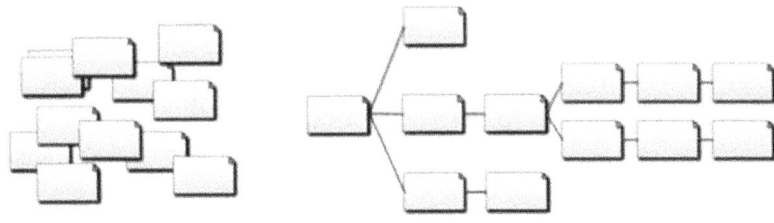

Random Collection of Processes        Organized Set of Processes

============================================================

Bill Flury

# CONTENTS

| | |
|---|---|
| A Practical Approach to Process Improvement | 1 |
| Introduction | 3 |
| Discover Your Process | 9 |
|    Step 1 - Select a Process | |
|    Step 2 - Gather Your Experts | |
|    Step 3 – Draw What You Do | |
| Find and Fix Every Flaw | 17 |
|    Step 4 - Add, Change, and Delete Steps | |
|    Step 5 - Track Performance | |
| Get On The Path To Maturity | 25 |
|    Step 6 - Make Process Improvement Continuous | |
|    Step 7 - Build a Process Improvement Process | |
| Post Logue | 35 |
| Attachments | 37 |
|    Tangible Benefits of Having a Well-Defined Process | |
|    Further Reading | |
|    Process Improvement Motivation – Or Lack Of It | |

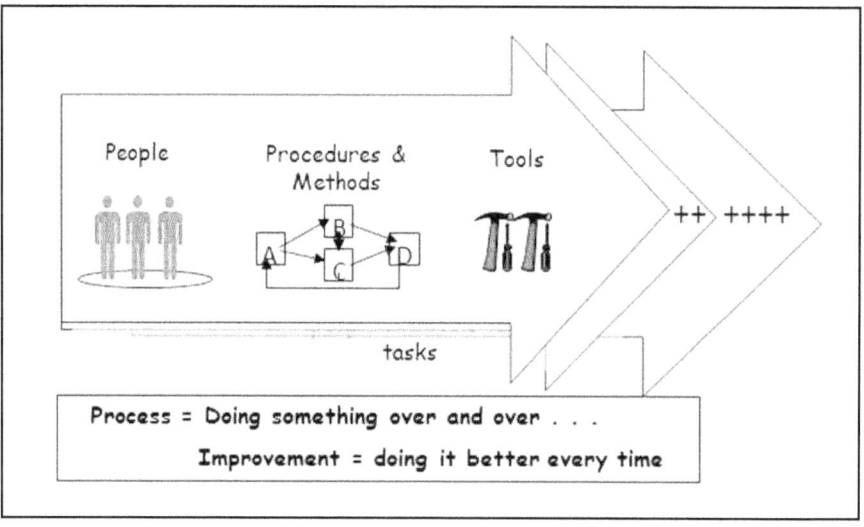

# A Practical Approach to Process Improvement

### Are You Having Fun Yet?

Do you arrive at work every morning knowing what you have to do today and knowing everything you need to succeed will be there when and where you need it? Do you work through the day with no hassles or crises? Do you go home on time, free to do whatever you want to do in the evening, with nothing left hanging over from today's assignments? Is every day like this where you work? And at home, does everything run perfectly smoothly? If this is the way it is for you, you can stop here.

If, on the other hand, your day-to-day activities at work or at home are beset with surprises, crises, delays, misunderstandings and other forms of headaches, keep reading. As they say in the headache ads, "Relief is on the Way."

### These are Your Process Headaches, Your Problems

You should read this because, it's about you and the things you do – the processes in which you are involved and the way you do them. Everything you do repeatedly in your life is a process and you are involved in lots of processes. It's time for you to get those processes better organized.

At work, you are involved in processes that: deliver products or provide services; change existing things; perform and report on analyses; prepare designs; conduct and report on tests; provide training; and much more. When your processes don't work smoothly you have crises. You have to stay late and miss your kid's swim meet, or you get unwanted phone calls while on vacation – and all those other things that you put up with that rob you of joy and give you headaches. Those are process headaches.

At home, there are processes that you execute every day: e.g., you make breakfast; you dress for work or school. There are other processes you do at home on an occasional basis: e.g., you mow the lawn; you do the laundry; you change the furnace filters. At home, when things go awry you have other types of crises and headaches (e.g., your supply process malfunctions and you run out of toilet paper). Those are all process headaches.

**Your Biggest Process Risk**

But, there can be even a bigger issue than just your personal process headaches at home or at work. You have much more at stake if your organization's processes don't work smoothly. If your processes at work don't perform well, your company won't do well. Clients may drop your company because of late or shoddy work. Competitors may pull ahead of your company. In some cases, potential clients may not even allow you to bid for work if you can't demonstrate consistent, reliable processes. So, if you fail to take action to make your processes work well, you can end up with a mega process headache – **no job!**

**It's Your Choice**

You can continue putting up with all those headaches, or you can take a few, simple steps to get your processes working better. Keep going to find out how to do that.

# INTRODUCTION

**Your Invisible Processes**

You know what you do but, if you were asked if you could describe it clearly to someone, how would you answer? If you are like most people you would likely answer – **"Well, sort of"**.

**"Well, sort of"** leaves lots of room for variations in what you do and each time you do it you may do things in a different sequence, forget to do a crucial part, or vary some other way.

Suppose you are going on vacation and want someone to do what you do while you are away. Would you be able to explain to someone clearly what has to be done? Would the substitute do things exactly as you do? Would the results be the same? If what you do is a critical task, would you be likely to get a phone call while you are at the beach?

Suppose you are working on a project with several others and you ask each person on the team to describe what the team is doing as a process, and everyone answers, **"Well, sort of."** Each person on the team will have a slightly different view of what is being done. That usually leads to delays and errors due to missed steps, redundant work, and out-of-sequence tasks. Does that happen in your team?

Most people can't very clearly describe what they do. They just do what they do. Then, when they have to do the same thing again, they just do it again based on what they *sort of* remember about how it went last time. They have no script to follow except their memory of what went before. Each time through the process is a new adventure – a new process – and the results vary each time.

In the business world, when everyone answers, **"Well, sort of"**, we call that chaos and working in chaos is no fun. If this is the way you or your organization works, keep reading because there is an easy way out of chaos.

**The Better Way**

Have you ever noticed the way the cast and orchestra of Broadway musicals operate? They have actors and musicians that all have to work together for the show to succeed. What provides the glue to keep all of the "players" from going their own independent direction? What keeps them working effectively and efficiently to produce a consistent product?

The key is that their process for delivering the show is documented in the score and libretto, the music and words for the show. Having learned these and practiced them as a group, the actors share a common vision and each individual knows what s/he needs to do to accomplish the common purpose. All the individuals have *clearly defined roles*.

Through their discussions at rehearsals, each individual comes to know precisely how he or she fits into this plan. The players know when to come in, how to do their part, and when to exit. They not only know what part they play, but they also know *how their part interacts with other players*. Trust is very important at this point. Each member of the team must trust the others to carry out their individual responsibilities. At show time, the conductor makes sure that all the players stay in sync with the script throughout the show.

If each team member does what is expected, the show moves smoothly and many repeat performances – all exactly the same – can result. If performers just *sort of* follow the script their variations may cause the carefully crafted magic of the show to fall apart and the show will flop.

The score and libretto are process documents. They define the process that the team will follow to put on the show. If you want your work to run as smoothly as a Broadway show you need to create your own version of the music and words and make sure that everyone follows both.

### That's just the first part. There's more.

If you define and document your processes like the theater folks do, you can run your shows through many performances and the results will be consistent. If things are working properly, when one of your actors gets ill your show can still go on with a substitute filling in. You have a defined, robust process at work. However, things always change so you have to find ways to update your process.

The Broadway folks have solved that problem also. On their way to Broadway they try out early versions of their script in New Haven or Peoria. As their test audiences and critics find flaws in the show the Director brings together the people who can help figure out how best to respond to the criticism with some improvements. In the next few performances they try some of those things and, if they work, they change the music and the script. That's a good example of process improvement.

You need to work like this, too. You can do the first part by preparing your music and your words (i.e., defining your processes and getting everyone to play). Then, you set up a process to conceive, try out and make orderly changes on a continuous basis and your show will continue to improve.

### What You Can Do

Here's your situation. You have some processes that are giving you headaches and you would like to make them work like the Broadway show model. However, your processes are only defined inside your head and the heads of your co-workers. You have two challenges:

> **Challenge # 1 --** How can you extract all those individual **"Well, sort of"** descriptions and get everyone to agree on a single version? You need to find a good, practical way to make your process visible to all so you can all see it and share ideas on how to make it work better.

**Challenge # 2** – How can you set up a process that will help you continually improve your processes? You need to develop a process improvement process and culture.

There are some easy ways to meet these challenges so you can put a stop to your headaches and start enjoying what you do. Many groups have made the transition. They have gone from chaos to fun in a very simple and straightforward way.

**Two Groups That Found a Way**

Let me tell you about two groups that had process headaches just like yours. They cured them by doing just a few simple things, things that you can do, too. They both began their work toward improvement by drawing a picture of what they were doing.

**Group One -- Curing Inconsistencies and Errors Headaches**

This group makes daily changes to a large database. They used to be plagued by errors in the delivered changes. We asked them to draw a picture of their process to see if they could figure out where the errors were coming from. When they tried to draw the picture of their process they found that everyone was doing changes in a different way and that was causing the errors. They finally agreed on one way to do changes and posted a picture of the agreed process on the wall for all to see. It is a complex process. The picture is 15 feet long.

On our last visit, they had a proud sign above the process picture that said, **"Number of Days Since the Last Delivery Error = 105"**. No one there has had to work overtime to do any re-work since the day they drew the picture and agreed to follow that process.

**Group Two – Curing Schedule Headaches**

This group does highly specialized printing for ad agencies. They were having frequent problems with delays that caused them to miss the time window for the ad agencies' programs. Their work involved careful coordination four separate teams: design, ink, paper, and press to provide truly unique advertising products.

First, they all agreed that they had to fix their process so they could do a better job of meeting deadlines. We got them together and had each person describe to the group how they thought their process worked. One member of the group worked at the whiteboard to capture what was being said. There were many differences in the descriptions of what should be put on the whiteboard and, as the differences came up, they were all recorded.

They discovered that each unit was working to its own schedule and that their schedules were not being coordinated with everyone concerned. Delays were being caused by unforeseen mismatches of ink and paper, design and ink, or ink and press. It quickly became apparent what the problem was and what they needed to change.

They agreed on a way to coordinate their materials ordering and testing schedules that would substantially reduce the time needed for testing. Then, they drew a new version of their picture to reflect that.

**Life After Headaches**

Both groups noticed improvements almost immediately. In the first group there were far fewer errors. Schedule slips became less frequent in the printing group. Their performance was now pretty consistent but both groups recognized that they could do even better. They also recognized that their process pictures would have to change from time-to-time as their client and suppliers changed.

The group doing database changes now keeps their process picture posted on the wall in their hallway. A pack of Sticky Notes is in a holder at the bottom. Anyone with an idea for how to make the process work better jots down the idea and puts it on the picture for all to see and add their comments.

Both groups now have regular, once-a-month, Brown Bag lunch meetings where they discuss potential improvements and agree on whether or not to change their picture. In these gatherings they also re-affirm that they will be careful to follow the processes because that's the only way they can tell if they are really working.

So, about their headaches – they don't have very many anymore. Ask anyone in either group what has changed since they drew their picture. They say it in lots of different ways, but their answer always comes out – **"Now our work is more fun."**

**How You Can Cure Your Process Headaches**

The approach laid out in this book will help you get started. It describes the steps that you should follow for each process you select and address. This practical approach to process improvement is simple. It does not take a lot of time or effort and, as you have seen from the two examples, **it works.**

# DISCOVER YOUR PROCESS

You already have processes in place. They are what you do. The problem is, you can't see them. You can't all see all the parts at once and you can't see how they all fit together.

Sure, everybody has a clear picture in their head of what they do **"Well – sort of"**. But even in the most dedicated and cohesive groups there can be significant differences in understanding "how we do things". That's a situation we call "Organized Chaos". Everyone knows exactly what they should do in executing the process but what everybody knows is slightly different. That's the situation this first part of the effort is designed to overcome.

You start by selecting one of the processes you want to work on. Choose one and get together with the rest of the people who are involved in it. As you talk you will discover that there are significant differences among those involved about how some aspects of the process are being performed.

You need to make the process visible so you can expose those differences and resolve them. Everyone who is involved needs to see the whole story. They all need to have a true picture of the process and how it really works now – warts and all.

Your primary objective here is to reveal and document the basic process and all its current variations to establish a baseline for future improvement. When you have finished this for any process you will have discovered and documented your process and will be ready to start improving it.

# Step 1: Select a Process

Choose a process to be addressed. If you are just starting process improvement you should start with a small process (e.g., responding to software change request, handling a "Hot Line" call). Once you can handle improving a simple process, you can tackle more complicated ones.

Here are some suggested selection criteria:

- ☐ The process is well-known and has visibility in your organization
- ☐ It occurs often enough to be observed and documented.
- ☐ A clear start and end can be defined
- ☐ It causes you some bothersome headaches
- ☐ Other people will also appreciate it if the process is improved
- ☐ Required changes can be put into effect with little or no outside help
- ☐ The others involved are willing to work on it with you

Next, you need to define where the process starts and where it stops. This will set the outer limits for your improvement effort. As an example, consider the process by which a software change request is processed:

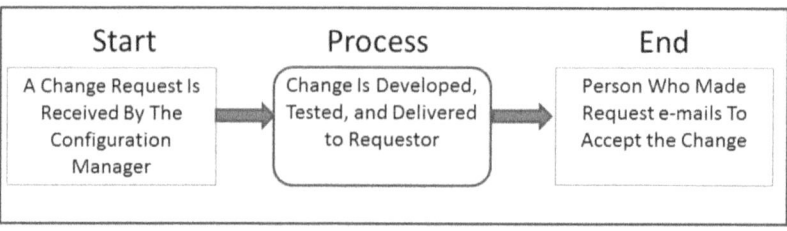

There are two things to remember. Don't try to do too much and make sure that your Start and End situations are tangible and clearly defined.

## Step 2: Gather Your Experts

To be effective, you will need to work with other people who know the workings of the process. Let's refer to them as your experts. Depending on the nature of the process, they may come from different departments, divisions, work centers, or offices. Everyone you get to help should be closely involved in the process you have selected.

You will have to arrange for a time and place to do the work involved, and the materials required. You may need to get some management approval to do this, especially if your experts are coming from different teams. Then, you will have to ask your experts to all to come and work with you in a few one or two hour meetings – maybe at a series of Brown Bag lunches. Ideally, they will approach this as an opportunity to cure their own headaches, rather than as extra work.

From experience we know that if you invest just 2 hours a week (i.e., 5%) of your time working on process improvement you will recover that amount of time and more within a few months. If you are working a 60 hour week that's only a 3% investment to get you headed back to a 40 hour, no headaches schedule.

If any of your experts are completely new to process improvement you might ask them to read this Book. Some other books are listed in "Further Reading at the end. One of those, *What Lucy Taught Me*, Is a short story about how a company operating in Chaos found a way to emerge and become effective again. You and your experts might find the situation described there is very similar to your own.

===========================================================
*We are all experts in our own little niches.*
**Alex Trebek**
===========================================================

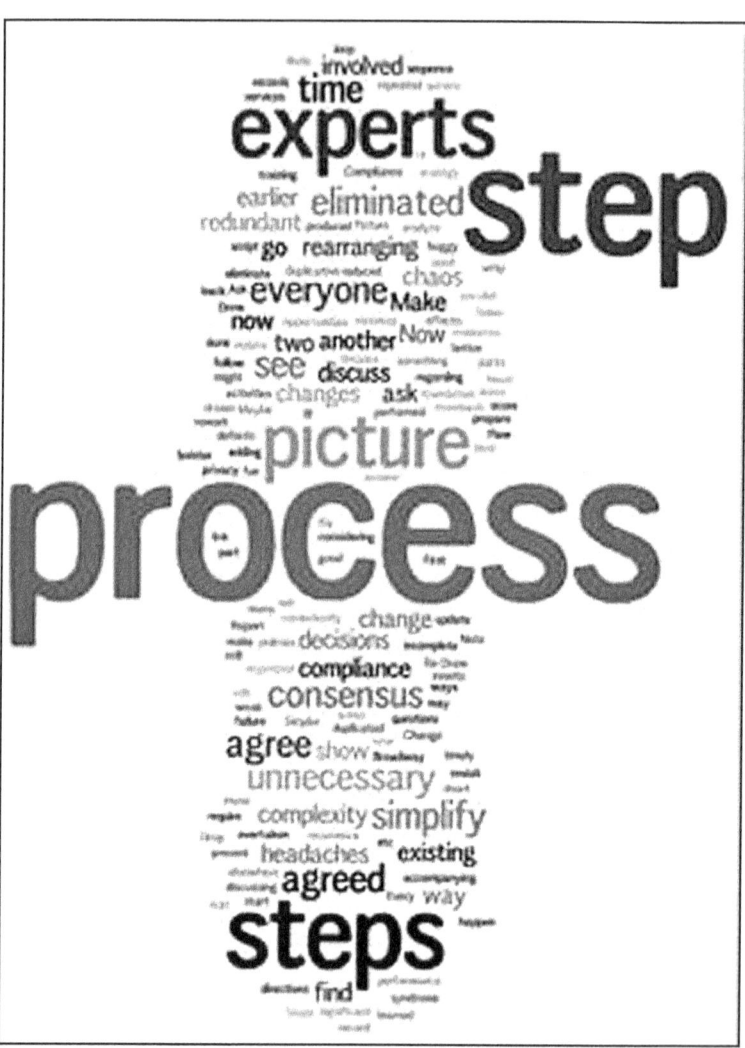

## Step 3: Draw What You Do

Before you can improve a process you have to be able to see how it works. You can't improve something you can't see. An American editor once said, "The best thing about writing something down is that then you can change it." In this step we will finally expose the process for all to see – and eventually change.

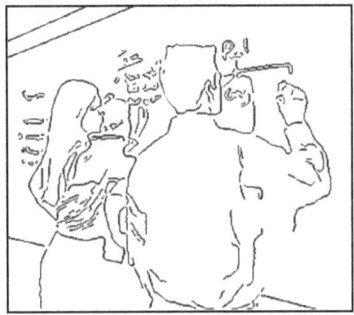

This is a job that you can't do on a computer screen or a piece of 8.5.x 11 paper. This requires some significant visual space. So, get a **BIG** piece of paper or a long whiteboard and get started. Get out your marker pens and your eraser and start drawing what you do. That will ultimately include a step-by-step picture of the activities, actions, and decisions that occur between the starting and stopping points of the process.

Each of your experts will be coming to this with his or her own idea of how this process works. Each knows a lot about what s/he does but may not know very much about how that interacts with what others do. You need to facilitate their conversation and interaction to draw out the picture of how the process is really being performed at present. You and your experts may need to walk through the flow of activity through the process several times before you all can see and draw the picture of what actually occurs.

As you work on this, you need to be careful to depict what is really happening in the process. There will be differences. Do your best to document them. Don't fall into the trap of drawing how people think the *process should work*, how *they would like it to work*, or how an instruction or *manual says it should work*. Only an as-is picture that displays the process as it is actually working today can serve as a proper base for making the improvements that may be needed. [No one is wrong but each has a different perspective.] By the end of this step you should have reached consensus on what is involved in the current process and how it works – now.

## Process View

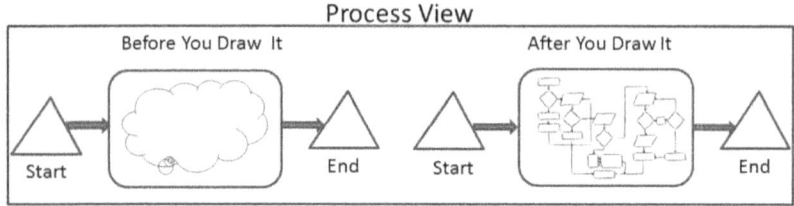

This record of where actions are taken, decisions are made, inspections are performed, and approvals are required becomes the "as-is" picture. It may be the very first accurate and complete picture of the process from beginning to end ever seen by any of the people who helped you create it.

The following example shows a high level view of the process for an on-line credit card sales transaction. Even this simple transaction involves many elements of the organization. The order is received by Sales, accepted by Finance, checked against the Inventory Control data base, then confirmed and acknowledged by Sales. Exceptions in the process are handled by a separate Control Group. Experts from each group should be included in the drawing process and subsequent discussions to add the detail required for full understanding.

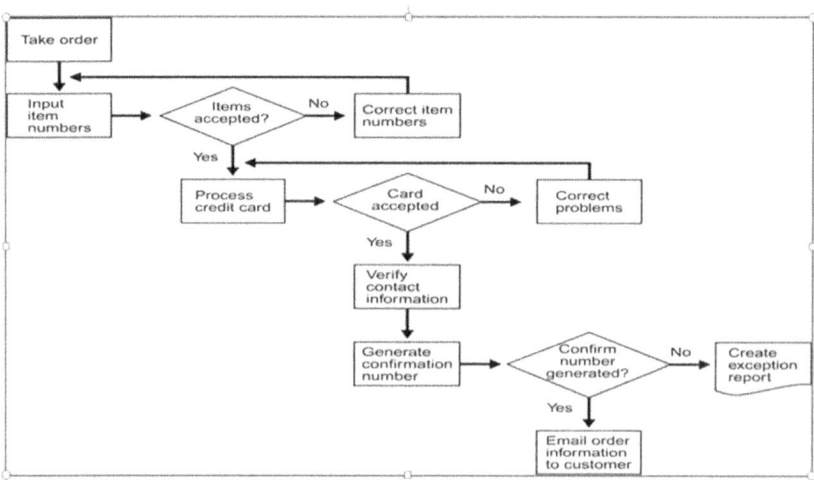

## What have you accomplished so far?

When you finally have the picture you have made the process visible to all concerned. That, in itself, is a very valuable achievement. The process is no longer an unseen, **sort of "ghost"**. Everyone can see the same picture and you can start to work together to improve it.

To find out if the work in this step is really complete you need to ask yourself and your experts:

*<u>Does this picture tell the truth, the whole truth, and nothing but the truth?</u>*

===========================================================

- ☐ We agree. We can move on to the next Step.
- ☐ We don't agree. Keep working on it until it accurately describes what we are doing now.

===========================================================

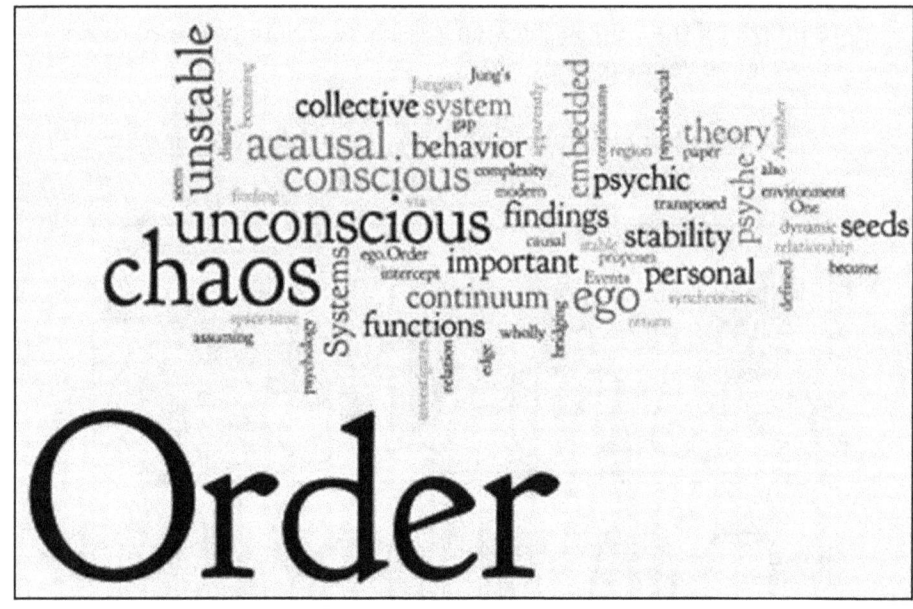

**What Are You Thinking About ?**

# FIND AND FIX EVERY FLAW

## Step 4 – Add, Change, and Delete Steps

If you did the earlier steps correctly you have a record of what you are presently doing. Now that you have a picture of the process that you can all see you can begin to edit to improve on the As-Is process.

In this step, you analyze the existing process to see if there are ways to simplify it by omitting unnecessary or duplicative steps or by rearranging steps to eliminate delays or minimize complexity. When you find opportunities for improvement you will discuss with your experts how you can work those in.

**Drop What You Don't Need**

First, you should discuss how you might simplify the process picture by removing redundant or unnecessary activities. Ask yourself and your experts: Is this step **necessary**?

- ☐ Does the step add value to the product or service produced by the process?
- ☐ What would happen if this step were eliminated?
- ☐ Would the output be unacceptable because it would be incomplete or have too many defects?
- ☐ Is this step required only because of another step that is being eliminated?
- ☐ Has this step been overtaken by events? (i.e., buggy whip syndrome)
- ☐ Is this step **duplicated** elsewhere in the process?
- ☐ Is the step a single repeated action, or is it part of a rework loop which can be eliminated?

If you all agree that something should be removed, change the picture. (Note: All decisions regarding changes should require consensus.)

## Make It Simpler

Next, you should see if you can simplify the process. You should ask, "Can the **complexity or length of the process** be reduced by combining or rearranging steps?"

- ☐ Can this step be done in parallel with other steps, rather than in sequence?
- ☐ Is the step a work-around because of poor training or a safety net inserted to prevent recurrence of a failure?
- ☐ Does this step have to be completed before another can be started, or can you combine steps?

## Make it Stronger

Besides identifying areas where resources are being wasted, you and your experts may find a weak link in the process that they can bolster by adding one or more steps.

## Check Compliance

If you were to change the process as you have been discussing, will the process still be in full compliance with all company policies and standards? What about security, privacy, confidentiality, records management, etc.? Will your recommended revisions violate any of these? Maybe you had better go back and check those aspects.

## Re-Draw the Picture

After considering all the changes in the picture of the process, you should prepare a new version of the picture and update all the accompanying notes. Then, you need to achieve consensus on the answer to these two questions. So, ask your experts:

- ☐ **Will the process, as drawn, consistently produce good, timely products or services in compliance with applicable existing directives?**

- ☐ **Will this make our headaches go away?**

If, at this point, you do not have consensus, it's time to revisit the earlier decisions and their effects on the process. If you and your experts all agree you can start to **Do What You Drew**.

**Progress Report**

You and your experts have now agreed on what you all agree is the "best way". It includes no unnecessary or redundant steps and everyone involved has agreed to follow that process as described in the picture. The process is now very likely to be more efficient – with fewer headaches and more fun.

To continue the Broadway show analogy, you have agreed on the score and the script, the players (your experts) have learned their parts and it's show time. Before, when everyone was improvising, it was chaos. Now, everyone involved can play from the same sheet of music. You have organized your way out of chaos and have established a foundation for consistent performance.

## Congratulations! That's a very significant achievement.

======================================================
*Coming together is a beginning; keeping together is progress; working together is success.*
**Henry Ford**
======================================================

## Where is the problem?

Process is being followed but not working well
- Important steps were omitted
- Process was poorly defined
- Outside influences not considered

### It's the Process

Process is <u>Not</u> being followed
- Not adequately staffed
- Staff not properly trained in the process
- Incentives for use lacking

### It's the Process

### It's <u>Always</u> the Process

---

"*Measurement is the first step that leads to control and eventually to improvement. If you can't measure something, you can't understand it. If you can't understand it, you can't control it. If you can't control it, you can't improve it.*"

— H. James Harrington

## Step 5: Track Performance

Now that you have drawn the process and posted it for all to see, you are ready to consider following it. From here on you will be following the process and seeing how it works.

Before, when the process was being performed in widely variable ways it made little sense to track performance because it was so random. Now that the process is defined and standardized, you can begin to develop a few performance  measures against which you can gauge the value of future process improvements. You should focus on just collecting the basic performance measures. These will be tallies of cost, schedule, and quality performance.

When you are deciding what data to collect, observe the "Goldilocks Rule". What you collect must be: "Not too much; not too little; but JUST RIGHT." As you start to work with the new process, track three aspects:

**How much effort is required to complete the process?**

If you keep track of the effort involved each time you execute the process you can determine:

- How much effort (e.g., staff hours) it usually takes to perform the process
- Least amount of effort (when things go well)
- Longest amount of effort (when things go poorly)
- How much variation there is in the amount of effort needed

If your time sheets are set up with codes that track to specific processes you can use them to provide the data for this. If the time sheets aren't set up for that you may have to ask the participants to keep track of their time as they do the work.

**How long does it take from start to finish (e.g., days, weeks)**

- Least amount of time (when things go well)
- Average amount of time
- Longest amount of time (when things go poorly)
- How much variation is there in the amount of time needed

You can use your project management tracking to keep track of how the process is performing against the schedule. Knowing this information will help you in planning future executions of the process and help you avoid those old time crunch headaches.

**How is the process performing in respect to quality?**

If your process includes reviews and quality checks you can count and record the number and location in the process of the noted flaws or faults. Another thing you can track is the amount of rework that is being done. (Remember the Group 1 Example, earlier.) The results will provide clues to where the process is not working as well as could be hoped. These are indicators of poor process quality and may signal a need to revisit the process design.

Save all your tracking data. Everything you collect will help you judge the potential costs and benefits of future proposed process improvements.

**Assessing Variations in Performance**

You are striving to achieve process consistency. What if the collected data show a wide range of variations in process performance? If you find this to be true you should investigate. Significant variations are possible indicators of subtle changes in the way people execute the process are likely to  occur without being noticed by the people performing the process.

There are two ways you may discover such changes. You can do periodic audits of process performance, stepping through the process definition with the persons performing the process.

The other way is to watch for changes in the performance data. Minor changes in the process may produce enough variation to be evident when the data are analyzed. If you see any of these indicators, you should go back through the earlier steps. Your follow-on actions will be dictated by what you find that is causing the process variation.

If your tracking data show that the process is running consistently you have achieved one of the goals of process improvement -- consistent performance. That, in itself is valuable because you can now do better predictions of cost, schedule and performance.

Depending on the stability and capability of the process, you may continue on immediately to seek additional improvements now or schedule the process to be considered again at a future date.

# The Process of Process Improvement is Continuous

# GET ON THE PATH TO MATURITY

## Step 6 – Make Process Improvement Continuous

Get started with guidance from a very well-known authority:

> *Good, Better, Best -- Never let it rest*
> *'Til the Good is Better – and the Better, Best*
> *- Mom*

That is good advice but Mom never really considered resource constraints. You have to decide: Have we done enough? Can we just set that process in stone and keep doing it as it is described? … or should we keep working on it? The answer is, as usual, "It Depends".

There could be other processes that you have not worked yet and you should consider them at this point. However, for simplicity, we will stay focused on the process on which you have been working so far.

When you are thinking about further improving a single process your decision regarding the amount of further improvement will be driven by one of the following:

-- Your monitoring shows that your process is performing poorly and needs fixing

-- There is a high probability of significant improvement in performance that would save time, lower costs or improve quality

What you have done so far is **Good** but pursuing **Better** and **Best** will take some effort. Any further action will be constrained by the resources available to do either or both of the above.

You should focus on just one dimension (i.e., Cost, schedule, or performance) at a time for iterations of your improvement efforts. Fixing flaws (e.g., Quality) in the process will always have a high priority but it should not completely eliminate your efforts to seek other, more general improvements. Whichever factor becomes the driver, you need to choose a specific goal to focus your efforts.

## Goal Driven Improvement

There is a familiar process you can follow to achieve continuous improvement. Starting with the process that you have already defined, the steps are much the same as when you first defined the process. You are going to Re-Do what you did in Steps 1 through 4. Now, however, you already have a picture of the process.

So, you can start by defining a specific improvement goal and then determine the best way to change the process to meet those goals. First, get agreement on the goal of the effort. *What improvement do we want to accomplish?* (e.g., reduce cost, shorten time, improve product quality) For an improvement effort to be successful, you must start with a clear definition of what you think the problem is and what you type and amount of improvement you expect to achieve.

As you saw with the example of the Group with the 15 foot process chart and the Sticky notes, opportunities for improvement can come in the form of suggestions by the people working in the process. They can identify activities that take too long, involve too many man-hours, include redundant or unnecessary steps, or are subject to frequent breakdowns or other delays. Their ideas need to be converted into actionable specific statements such as, **"I think we can reduce the time needed to prepare these reports by modifying steps 3 and 5 in the process."** Such statements will serve as tangible goals for the improvement process.

The next step is analysis. You have done this before. Put the picture up on the wall, and look for the causes of the problems and the sources of opportunities for improvement. Search for possible changes in the process that might help achieve the goal and select some to test for effectiveness. Find all the possible changes to the process that would achieve the stated goal.

If your effort is aimed at finding and fixing the parts of the process that cause flawed performance, be specific as to what types of flaws are the focus of your concern. These will be the types found in your process performance data (e.g., over-run schedules, excessive costs, returned products).

As you think about possible changes to the process you should also consider the resources that might be required to make the change. Ask these questions:

- ☐ What steps in the process will be changed?
- ☐ What workers will be affected by the change?
- ☐ What training or re-training will be required?
- ☐ Who will be responsible for implementing the change?
- ☐ What will the change cost? *(The cost includes not only money, but time, number of people, materials used, and other factors.)*
- ☐ Are there any risks associated with the proposed change?
- ☐ Is there a downside to the proposed change?
- ☐ Will any other processes be affected?

Next, evaluate all the possible improvements and their resource requirements and redraw your picture to incorporate all of the changes on which you have consensus.

You should then test your proposed version. The **easiest** way to check this is to do a peer review, a walkthrough on paper with some other folks who were not with you when you were doing the earlier work. The **best** way is to actually try doing the process, step-by-step as you laid it out. To do this, you should find some folks who have been doing the process and set them up to go through it a few times.

Continued tracking of your process performance will let you assess whether the change really improved the process. Has it really reduced the incidence of errors? Has it reduced costs or shortened schedules? Has it made the process more robust in dealing with changing conditions? Ask yourself, "Did the change meet the stated goal?" Let's hope the answer will be YES.

**If the answer isn't YES, you know what you have to do.**

# Step 7 – Build a Process Improvement Process

**"So Many Processes – So Little Time"**

After seeing the benefits you can achieve for one of your processes and (I hope) losing your fear of process improvement being too hard, you might want to advocate doing the same for all of your organizations' processes. If you want to do more you will need some help.

Working on many processes serially or at the same time is a demanding job that requires a dedicated, continuing effort and focused leadership. You should start thinking of this as a new, separate project – a project to create and operate a Process Improvement Process. This will provide a clear focus for the effort and will provide a mechanism for obtaining and applying the resources required.

You can start by getting yourself or some other highly motivated person designated to lead the effort. Then you need to assemble a few knowledgeable folks and develop a draft Project Plan. This working group will lay the groundwork for establishing an internal organization that will be the acknowledged leader in advancing the overall continual improvement of the organization's processes. [For convenience, let's refer to that organization as the Process Action Team.

Some goals you might recommend for the team are:
- Establish and oversee the operations of a process wherein those involved in each process will routinely share their knowledge and pursue improvements in an orderly and effective manner.

- Ensure that process performance is effectively monitored so that improvement results are properly recognized and rewarded.
- Ensure the timely collection and maintenance of all your process assets (e.g., process drawings, Lessons Learned, performance tracking data)
- Ensure that everyone receives proper training in process improvement principles, and methods

Since the Process Action Team will be working as an internal project, you will have to develop a plan for its establishment and operation. You will also have to consider all the usual things your project management courses have stressed:

**Scope – Time – Cost of the Project**
- How many processes will be addressed?
- Will processes be addressed serially or in combinations?
- How will action priorities and schedules be set?
- Who will do the work?
- What resources will be required?

**Mode of operation**
- How will the project team be organized?
- When and where will they convene to do their work?
- How will they facilitate improvements?
- What will be their role in implementing improvements?
- What will be their role after improvements are made?

**Record Keeping**
- What documents and data will need to be collected and maintained?
- How will these be stored and accessed?
- How will their use be encouraged and facilitated?

**What Comes Next**

Once you have your plan it will be time to get it approved by your management and put it into action. You will need to follow your organization's process for planning, budgeting, reviewing, and approving internal projects.

If you have been through the process once on your own you should be able to make a pretty good case for implementing your plan. You should be able to cite the specific improvements you have accomplished with your first effort and the amount of time it took to achieve them. Be sure to develop a good "Elevator Speech" that you can use to promote the project.

**Now, Get To Work**

There are some sticky problems that you probably considered theoretically during the planning but now you and the Process Action Team have to address them for real.

**Problem # 1 – Lighting the Fire**

There are some people in your organization that don't care about process improvement (gasp!). There are others who harbor gross misunderstandings about what it is and how it will affect them and their work. A description of the situations that lead to such attitudes is presented in Attachment 3. That Attachment also includes advice on how to convince those with such attitudes that they really can benefit by actively participating in your process improvement activities.

**Problem # 2 – Adding Fuel to the Fire**

In many organizations the recognition and rewards tend to flow to the "heroes", the ones who "worked nights and weekends to get the job done." From a process improvement standpoint, it would be wonderful if you could change the system so it would identify and recognize people who did their process well and did NOT have to work nights and weekends to get the job done. If you can do that you will greatly improve your chances for success.

**Problem # 3 – Watching Out For Pitfalls**

Your fellow workers' lack of interest in process improvement (See Problem # 1) is not the only thing that threatens your success. There are many other potential pitfalls.

**Dithering** - Trying to multi-task your way into the planning effort is a good example. Trying to fit in development of the plan while you are very actively involved in other project can stretch the time to complete the plan. By the time you are done everyone has lost interest and the fire you hoped to kindle will probably have died out.

**Resource melting** – In busy organizations resources assigned to a project tend to melt. The runoff goes to other projects that are deemed more important. You have to work hard to maintain the level and type of resources you need to do the work as planned.

**Vision problems** – As it happens with people, vision fades with age. You need to have you vision checked periodically and get your prescription updated.

**Re-Planning** – Things change! People, projects, and processes change and you will need to re-plan your process improvement program on a regular basis. A six-month cycle would probably be good enough.

**Training** – You will always be told by management that they can't afford the training you and your co-workers need for your process improvement efforts to succeed. You need to remind them of two facts: (1) process improvement doesn't really cost that much if you do it as we have presented in this Book; and (2) continuing to operate with inefficient processes costs everyone a lot more than what you are asking for.

**Process Rust** – As processes age, they tend to erode, much as rust erodes iron and steel. Without regular reminding, people following the process tend to drift off into the **"Well, sort of"** mode that we mentioned at the beginning. Our example Group 1 found the answer for this. They not only posted the drawing of their process in a hallway that everyone used every day, they actively challenged everyone to use the Sticky Notes to make suggestions. No rust accumulates on their process.

===========================================================

*Draw what you do, do what you draw*
*Find and fix every flaw*

*Track Performance to ensure*
*You're on the path to be mature.*

*(Repeat as necessary)*

===========================================================

Bill Flury

# POST - LOGUE

**Are you having fun yet?**

Well, maybe not quite yet. But, now perhaps you can see a pathway you can follow to getting there. You get there by following systematic process improvement methods and practices.

You know full well about the crises that occur and headaches that result at work when things don't go right. Hopefully, you have come to understand that fixing crises as they occur (i.e. firefighting) is a never ending task and you need to take a more systematic approach (i.e. fire-prevention) to provide lasting relief.

In this Book we have tried to increase your awareness of the problems you and your co-workers face in fixing your processes. We accept the fact that everyone wants to do a good job and make the processes work well. However, we also recognize the difficulty you and your co-workers have in understanding how the things you do inter-relate. That is the greatest barrier you need to overcome on your pathway to fun.

Our proposed approach for dealing with that problem is simple. It requires a large drawing surface, good drawing tools (including erasers), and people willing to work together to find the path to take their process from chaos to fun. Then, just follow the path we have laid out.

**Still having crises and headaches? You know what to do.**

## It's time to get started.

## There Is Still More

There are a few Attachments of interest:

**Attachment 1** describes some very tangible benefits you can realize by having a big picture of your process posted in the place where you work.

**Attachment 2** lists many other books that are well worth reading. All are available either in stores or on-line.

**Attachment 3** was noted before and it provides insight and help on how to change attitudes regarding process improvement.

# ATTACHMENT 1

# Tangible Benefits of Having a Well-Defined Process

1. **You Avoid Doing Useless Work**

When your processes were being defined you looked for and eliminated useless work. If everyone involved in the process is following the process you should never find yourself doing work that is not useful. Remember the days when you were in chaos. You and someone else would sometimes be doing the same thing and finding out about it after you had spent time on it. Or, you would do something early in the process that would be obsolete by the time it was really needed and have to be redone. That stuff is now gone and you are no longer wasting time on it.

2. **You Have Fewer (if any) Crises**

With well-defined processes in place, you never have to worry about who does what or what comes next. The process steps are all laid out and you can trust everyone else to do what they are supposed to do when they are supposed to do it. That kind of certainty is a blessing. You don't have to work late to catch up because of things being left undone.

When the process is not defined, you can never be sure that everything required has been done. Here's where you get a big bonus. When all the process steps are checked off, you don't have to waste time going back over things to see if the job is complete. You know that you are done.

3. **Your Work is Scheduled More Realistically**

Project estimators are usually accused of being overly-optimistic or yielding to pressure to underbid the job. When the processes are not defined, every estimate is just a wild guess. That is, perhaps, the biggest cause of headaches for the staff that has to do the job. This is what turns their allocated 40 hours of time into a 60 hour work week. There's no fun here.

With good processes in place and being followed, estimators can see and estimate for all tasks involved in the job. Current performance data can provide a sound basis of estimate for jobs that are similar to others. Estimates can be very accurate when all steps in a process are accounted for and comparable performance data can be found and used. When estimates are made this way you can be confident that the estimated 40 hours of work can be done in 40 hours. No more uncompensated overtime.

4. **You Negotiate Your Schedule with Facts, Not Opinions**

When you already have a lot of work to do and your boss asks you to take on some new, urgent task you are defenseless if you don't have a defined process. You are in no position to describe what tasks you would have to put off in order to take on the new work. You sound really lame when all you can say is, *"Well, I'll have to put something else off to do that."* And the Boss says, *"What?"* – and you mumble your answer.

It's much better when you can take the Boss to your process chart and the two of you can discuss, in detail, how much effort the new task will require and then see, specifically, what portion of your current work will have to be put off to match the effort required for the new work.

5. **You Spend Less Time Training**

Fred Brooks in "The Mythical Man-Month", says adding people to a project running late will slow it down and make it even later. Why? Because the staff that was already working hard to meet the deadline would have to take time to train the reinforcements in the process. Think how much better it is when you have a picture of your process you can show the reinforcements. Then, instead of having to describe each step you can just be available for questions.

6. **You Get Your Non-Work Life Back**

Just think of the time you will save: No useless work or time wasted on crises
- No time spent to make up for underestimates
- No time spent in handling "urgent" along with regular work
- Less time spent in training

This could turn your 60 hour week into a 40 hour week. It's your call as to what you do with the saved time. While most of that should be applied to your non-work life you should also consider investing a few of those saved hours each week to think creatively about your work and how you can continue to improve what you do and how you do it.

7. **Bonus Benefit**

At every place we have seen processes defined and institutionalized and gone back later to ask "What has changed?" --- The answer is **always** ---

## "Our work is now more fun!"

# ATTACHMENT 2

# Further Reading

## Recent, Outstanding Books

**Interpreting the CMMI (R): A Process Improvement Approach,**
Margaret K. Kulpa, Kent A. Johnson, Second Edition (2008)

**The Economics of Software Quality**
Capers Jones, Olivier Bonsignour, (2011)

**What Lucy Taught Us: A Management Fable about Improving Your Business One Process at a Time,** Walter T. Geer, Jr. (2009)

**A Practical Guide to Information Systems Process Improvement,** Anita Cassidy, Keith Guggenberger, (2000)

**Continuous Process Improvement: The Quality Improvement Series (Practical Guidebook Collection): (Paperback),** Richard Y. Chang (1996)

## Classic Books on Process Improvement

**Handbook for Process Improvement:** This Handbook was originally issued by CINCPACFLT in 1992 and revised in 1996. The 1996 version can be downloaded from http://www.cpf.navy.mil/pages/n00qio/BPI%20Manual/Handbook.htm

**Out of the Crisis** (1982, 2003)
W. Edwards Deming

**Managing the Software Process** (1989)
Watts S. Humphrey

Also, See:

**CMMI Institute Books at:** http://cmmiinstitute.com/


More about this book at: http://www.DrawWhatYouDo.com

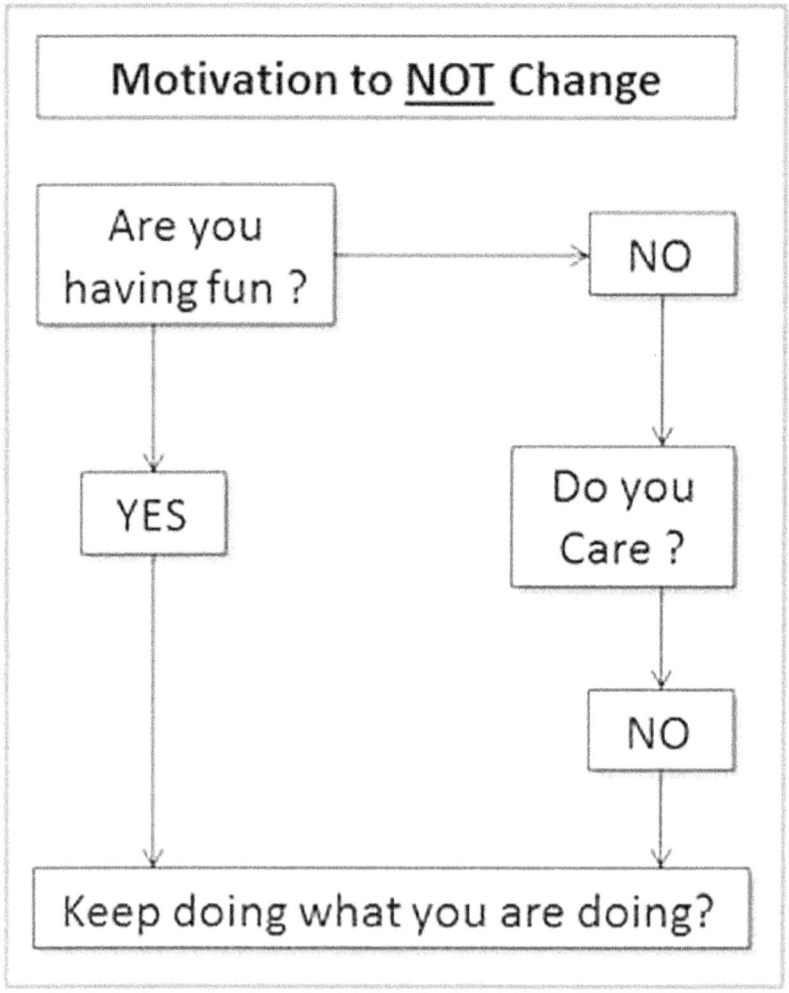

# ATTACHMENT 3

# Process Improvement Motivation -- Or Lack of It

You would think that something that includes "Improvement" in the title is good and everyone should be in favor of it. However, it doesn't play out that way. There are people who just don't comprehend the need or feel that it would not be worth doing. And, there are some who fear it. Trying to force people with any of these attitudes into a process improvement program will almost always fail.

In order to succeed with a process improvement program you need to make sure everyone comprehends the benefits and costs to them – not only on a company level but also on a personal level. Without that, they will treat the program like bad tasting medicine. They will do their best to avoid the things they need to do to make it work. Let's look at the different types of motivation lack and think about how to deal with them.

**Workers -- "We're Doing Fine"**

Let's start with workers who just don't seem to care about Process Improvement. Ask them about doing something to improve their processes and they say, "We're doing fine. Don't bother us with that stuff."

These folks have mix-ups, make mistakes, and deliver their products late or with errors, but none of that is a problem for them or their company. So, why don't they care about that? Why doesn't all of that give them headaches? How can they feel that they are "fine" and don't need to improve the way they work?

There are several factors that combine to shape their lack of interest in improvement. Here's a software world example. The workers involved in this process develop, test and deliver software changes to a government IT system. They work under the terms of a services contract. They, and their company, get paid for all of the hours they work. That includes any time for extra work or rework before or after they deliver their products. It also includes payment for overtime when that is needed. In some contracts of this type there is premium pay for overtime and that is an incentive to create a need for it.

The workers have somewhat rare skills. They have had long-term experience with their client's IT system. They feel secure because it would be difficult for their client to replace them without a major disruption in their operations. The client cannot do the work with internal staff so the client is quite tolerant of mistakes, errors, and late deliveries.

There is never a deadline. The client's IT system has been in place for a long time and will continue for a long time to come. Changes are needed at a fairly steady rate and it is extremely rare to have a requirement to make a change by a certain date. When that does occur, other changes get deferred so the workload stays steady.

Another factor – the type of work these programmers do is similar to what auto mechanics do. Every job appears to be different and, in fact they are. However, the process that they follow in attacking each job and making the changes always includes the same kinds of tasks: analyze the problem; devise a change; write the "fix"; test the fix; deliver the change; and adjust the documentation. There is enough similarity in those jobs to make it possible to do them better, cheaper and faster – if one really wanted to. But, why?

The work allows little opportunity for recognition. With no regular measurement of performance, management has no way to recognize and reward good performance. The workers get their psychic income form their peers. They know who is the "best" and that's enough for them.

So, from the workers' standpoint, what's to improve? They work at a pace that suits them and get paid for every hour they work. They get paid for good work or bad. If they have to work overtime (for any reason) they get a premium. Their management is not concerned about the pace of their work because they can bill for every hour – and more is better. The client tolerates this because they have no other options.

They're "fine". But, are they, really? What if the company loses its permissive client and has to compete for work with one that is really concerned about cost, schedule and technical performance? On personal level, what if the company can't compete and the workers need to find other jobs. What will they have to show for their past performance? Maybe they should care.

**Managers – "It's not required."**

These are managers who do not perceive the Return on Investment of Process Improvement. They have clients who don't care either. As noted above, some clients really do not have any concern about cost, schedule or performance. (Don't tell THEIR bosses that.) When the client doesn't really care there is no perceived value to the company to try to improve on current performance.

With no meaningful data on current productivity or performance, it is hard to perceive how working differently (better) would make the company more competitive in a services Time & Materials environment. Competition has to be on cost alone. No case can be made for productivity per hour. The company is just selling hours – good or bad are all the same price.

The only real incentive to undertake a process improvement program in this environment is when the client requires formal certification of the company processes. This requirement forces the company to undertake a formal certification in order to continue to do business with the client.

(Note: When the client also does not have a process improvement program such a mandate is usually in response to a demand from above that is targeted at contractors. As a result, the client is often satisfied with pro forma satisfaction of the certification requirements.)

No one likes to be forced to take on a process improvement program. It is even worse when you don't have a clue as to the costs and benefits, the Return on Investment of the program.

**Everyone – "It's too complicated and costs too much."**

Unfortunately, the jargon and complexity of the formal process improvement programs are hard to understand and tend to confuse people. Process improvement consultants stress rigor and company managers often overreact to the advice. This leads them to misperceive and vastly overestimate the cost of putting a formal program into action. Already leery of the potential benefits, company managers approach the process improvement programs with great concern. Without being required to do such a program, few could be convinced of the value.

# How to Change Attitudes Regarding Process Improvement

Getting a process improvement program into operation and working well is not easy. You have to overcome some inertia – the feeling that "We're fine, why should we change what we're doing? Well, there are some reasons. The willingness to do process improvement varies for each of these reasons.

**Motivating Managers**

There are three basic reasons managers might want to develop and implement a process improvement program. All are aimed at improving performance.

**Reason # 1 – Process Inconsistency Problems** – If they have been having problems with crises, missed schedules, cost overruns or defective products they will want to find and fix the process problems that cause these. All of these problems are vexing and most, ultimately affect their bottom line or performance reputation. *The first part of process improvement is to establish performance consistency.*

**Reason # 2 – Competition** – In a competitive world you always has to do its best in order to keep up with or get ahead of the competition. Even if things are going well they can always be done better and a formal process improvement approach will help do that. *Setting up to do continuous improvement is the second part of a sound process improvement program.*

**Reason # 3 – Some Customers Require It** – Some present and potential customers are aware of the fact that companies that have effective process improvement programs actually perform better than those that do not. They have chosen certification standards (e.g., CMMI®, ISO, Six Sigma) and now require that bidders meet these standard in order to qualify to do business with them. To do business with these customers your company has to be able to prove that it has an effective process improvement program in place and operating. Achieving such certifications requires that you be able to demonstrate that you are doing parts one and two, above. If you can't meet the standards you can't play.

## Motivating Workers

For managers the motivation is pegged to how the company performs. For workers, it's all about them – their problems and frustrations and headaches – if they have any. Here are some approaches that can be used to convince them to support the process improvement program.

### "It's More Fun" Approach --

For a testimonial from a guy who left a company with a good process improvement program and is now in a company without a program, see below:

```
==============================================================
        Subject: Work
        From: davidz@mcs.com
        To: techldr@raycom.com
        Date: Mon, 26 Mar 2001 15:58:00 -0600

        After working for a company that went from chaos to process, process has
        become an expectation. It's like getting a faster machine, and then changing
        employers and working with a slower machine.

        I'm back working in chaos, and a rare day goes by where I don't notice the
        difference.
        David
==============================================================
```

When the processes are inconsistent work is no fun. Things get left undone or done poorly or late and people can get upset by the crises and the need to work late to fix problems or the other signs of process disarray. When it gets bad enough, some may want to make things work more smoothly – but may not know how a process improvement program can help and how easy it can be. You have to explain both of those things to them and, even then, they may still think it's too hard and not worth the effort. So, you've got to be really convincing.

**"We'll be out of business if we don't" Approach**-- Losing a few bids because your company's costs were too high or your references said that your work has been faulty or late can provide a bit stronger motivation for process improvement. This is an easier sell because you can target specific problems (e.g., late deliveries, returned products) as process problems that need to be fixed so you can compete better.

However, even if your company has been competing well you have to remember the old Satchel Paige quote: "Never look back, they may be gaining on you." Don't forget, your competitors also know about process improvement and are practicing it. To stay competitive you always have to do better.

**"The Customer says we have to" Approach** -- This last reason is the hardest sell. When you tell the staff that they have to do all that is necessary to get certified you get the reaction, "Gee, Mom, do I have to?" So, yes, you have to. Your job depends on it. It is a Do or Die situation.

The good news is that the medicine can be made to taste pretty good and, if you have been doing process improvement for a while getting certified is not too hard – because you will have been doing all the things that are required.

## Motivation -- Bad Things to Avoid

You have to make sure that none of the "killer Attitudes" takes root in your organization. Find ways to make sure no one ever says:

- We are just doing this to get the certification.
- We can do this in our spare time.
- We'll do all the paperwork stuff but we'll still do it our way.
- Our tech staff doesn't have time to do this, let's have the new intern do it.
- We've been doing this for 20 years and we're still here – why change now?

## Motivation – Good Things to Have

### A Knowledgeable, Committed Senior Leader

An essential first step in getting started on process improvement is for you to get a senior leader to give you some time to do it and make it a priority. You have to be really convincing. You have got to make sure that your leader fully comprehends and believes in the concept of continuous process improvement and will provide the resources required to do it.

### Easy, Practical Methods For Implementation

Many companies have found simple, practical ways to implement their programs and have achieved the benefits with little cost. Every company already has a process in place. They key factor in keeping the improvement effort simple is to start with documenting what is already in place in way that all can share. From that point on, potential improvements can be identified, tried, installed, and documented on a continuous basis. That is simple, is not costly, and it is good business.

Process improvement efforts succeed when everyone understands and really cares.

- When the workers understand and really care
- When the managers really understand and really care
- When the clients really understand and care

If you can accomplish this you will have a successful program.

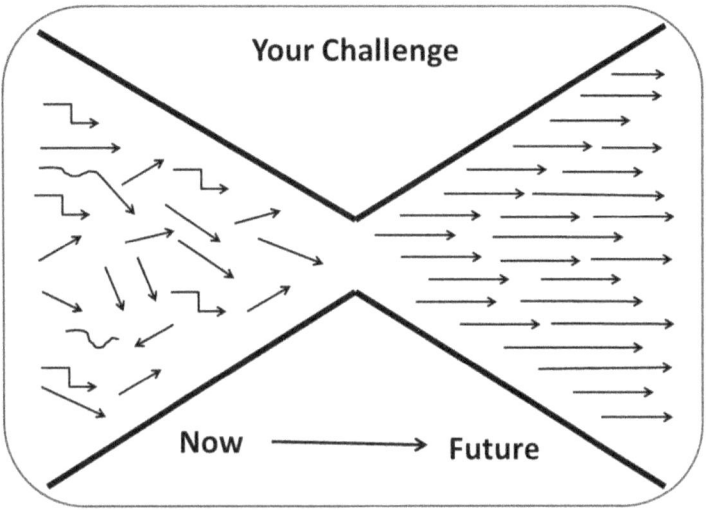

This is a WORDLE summary of the entire contents of the book.

## ABOUT THE AUTHOR

Bill is an independent consultant specializing in process improvement and project management. Prior to his retirement he worked as a project manager with MITRE Corporation and SRA International developing and implementing major government information systems. At SRA he managed 85 projects with a perfect cost, schedule and performance record.

Since retirement, Bill has taught project management and systems engineering for American University, Strategy Bridge International, GEMSOC, LLC, and the Center for Systems Management (CSM). At CSM he developed and ran a process improvement practice that has conducted over 100 process assessments. Bill continues to be a frequent facilitator of process improvement workshops for government agencies and development organizations.

**For the latest information, visit:**

http://www.DrawWhatYouDo.com

www.ingramcontent.com/pod-product-compliance
Lightning Source LLC
Chambersburg PA
CBHW071818170526
45167CB00003B/1361